AF230078

Turning Pages

The King's English at 40

Printed in the United States of America by
Ingram Spark

Table of Contents

Introduction

Our second annual anthology, *Turning Pages: The King's English at 40*, showcases the breadth and depth of our customers' creative talent, and it is considerable! Focusing on the theme, "Once Upon a Time in the Bookshop," contributors in two broad age groups submitted entries in three writing categories—fiction, nonfiction and poetry—and in the visual arts. The thoughtful and carefully crafted pieces collected here are a delight to experience. We think you'll agree, and it is our pleasure to share them with you.

Beginning with this volume, the *Turning Pages* anthologies will be published under our own imprint, TKE Ink. The new venture will allow us to foster the love of reading and writing on a more personal basis, and to identify and publish works of fiction and nonfiction that move us in a new and interesting ways.

Here's to 40. Here's to creativity.

Joni Butler Payne
Winner | Visual Arts

Tails of a Bookstore

Samuel Morse

Winner | Written Word (12 and under)

Once upon a time at the bookstore, there was a dog. The bookstore only had one dog but had many books about dogs. The dog's name was Perry. Perry enjoyed taking naps on his favorite reading chair, sniffing all the new books, but most of all, being read to.

In her spare time, the manager would read to him. Every day she would read him a new book. Sometimes the local children would come and read to him. Perry just loved a good story and all the attention. One of Perry's favorite parts of being read to was picking out which story to read. He would use the sniff test. You could tell if a book was good if it smelled like bacon, but if it smelled like broccoli, you'd better stay away. You can't tell a book by its cover, but you can tell a book by its smell.

When there was somebody to read to him, Perry loved it, but sometimes, when there wasn't anyone to read to him, he got lonely. The manager noticed this, so she adopted another dog.

The second dog's name was Sparky. At first, Perry didn't know what to think of Sparky. He was too shy to read to; he was super noisy, and his idea of peeing on books to make them smell better only got the dogs in trouble. Nevertheless, it was nice to have some company and, eventually, Perry warmed up to Sparky. He was fun to play with, but he still didn't like being read to, so Perry devised a plan to make him enjoy it.

First, Perry taught him how to find a good book. He found a book that he knew smelled good, then let Sparky decide if it was good or not. Perry then got the manager to read the book that Sparky liked. If Sparky heard the story and still liked the book, then Perry would move on to Step Two.

Step Two involved trusting anyone that wanted to read to you. Perry told Sparky that a big part of living in a bookstore is letting anyone read to you. He showed Sparky that he didn't need to be afraid of people. Perry made Sparky watch people read to him many times and showed Sparky that people weren't going to harm him. After the 50th person read to Perry, Sparky was ready.

Step Three was getting people to read to Sparky. Perry told Sparky that he had to be patient because some people were crazy and didn't want to read to dogs. He taught Sparky how to sit still and make cute puppy eyes to draw people over. He also told Sparky to have a book in front of him to tell people that he wanted to be read to.

Finally, someone came over and read to Sparky. Sparky was a little nervous at first, but by the end of the book, he had had a great time and barked to say, "Thanks."

By the end of the day, Sparky had been read to over 10 times. Perry was glad to see Sparky as happy as he had become once upon a time at the bookstore.

Aloo Govi

Hartman Macey

Winner | Written Word (13 and over)

For Mom

This embodies something Joan
referred to in a picture—Braunvieh.
You pronounce it slow like the brown cow
retired to the alps in your sister's
photograph; a cow eating wild grass
off of a mountainside.

Here we eat Indian food, a seance red
curtain light implodes, a sconce lantern
rounded, a beehive with a light,
we fan the menu quiet as the cow,
or the Swiss grass in the breeze, your sister's
grey fringe blows toward a stone bench.

We're here in a strip mall, we speak with
a young Pakistani waitress with a piercing
near the edge of her nose,
she takes down my vindaloo, you point to
aloo govi, she encourages you to say it,
your pronunciation is slow.

You show her the picture, your sister,
the cow, you surprise me sometimes,
you change directions, ask my thoughts
on the Montana wildfires, I recall a poem
by William Stafford, The Way It Is,
found once upon a time at a bookshop.

Once upon a time at the bookstore ...

Russ Isabella

Winner | Best Use of Theme

Once upon a time at the bookstore....

- My newlywed wife and I found an oasis of independence during our once-monthly sojourns to Salt Lake City from Logan, UT, where we had landed in 1986 as if onto another planet from parts far to the east of here;
- My pregnant wife and I and our two-year old son, relatively new transplants to Salt Lake City, came in out of the snow to join in our first of some 28 holiday parties;
- I received a wonderful recommendation from Barbara;
- My two young children visited with Santa;
- Ann Cannon patiently assisted my construction of a stack of books appropriate for my two young nieces;
- Betsy turned me on to a fantastic mystery;
- Another holiday party and a signed book by Pat Bagley
- I spent too much money at an annual sale;
- I had a star-struck moment meeting my favorite author;
- My children attended Saturday morning storytime;

- I feared the end of independence might be in sight and tried to do something about it;
- Another great read was placed into my hands by Kathy;
- My children lost themselves in the children's room;
- I lost myself in the mystery section;
- I was the first person through the door for an annual sale;
- Another stack of books for my nieces, this time with the help of Anne Holman;
- My children and I hung out until midnight when we were at the front of the line for the unboxing of the latest Harry Potter installment;
- Whitney turned me on to the wonderful world of the YA novel;
- Margaret helped me fill the gift bags for the youngest members of my ever-growing extended family;
- Claire shared her contagious joy for all things "children's books;"
- Betsy thanked me for attending TKE's birthday bash and recognizing this remarkable cornerstone of our community she (with a little help from her friends!) has so graciously and selflessly championed;
- I found a place as inviting, stimulating, comfortable and comforting as I ever could want it to be.

Thank you, TKE, for all that you have been and meant to me and to my family throughout the years. We were lucky to have settled so close to you, and we are luckier still to be a small part of your wonderful, sometimes wacky, and always loving independent world.

Customers Who Bought This Item Also Bought

Chaunceton Bird

$14.99? That's got to be two or three dollars more than on Amazon. And they don't have the hardcover in stock. Sure, they could order it, but so can I; probably for 25% less than what this place will charge me. Hmm. Well. Oh well. It's not like I need a book anyway. For $15 I could get two matinee tickets.

"Oh, my goodness, that book changed my life," says a stranger to my left. One look at this person and I can tell she's probably read everything in this store, except maybe some of the stuff in the Manga section.

"Really? I haven't read it," I reply, "of course I always hear the phrase 'Catch-22,' but I just haven't gotten around to reading it."

"Well, I envy the experience you are about to have as a first-time reader." Then, after a short pause, she asks, "have you read anything of Kurt Vonnegut's?"

"Kurt who?"

"Kurt Vonnegut, if you're interested in *Catch-22* I'm sure you would also enjoy *Slaughterhouse Five* and *Cat's Cradle* by Kurt Vonnegut. It was in Vonnegut's books that I learned fiction can be truer than nonfiction."

"Yeah, I guess so," is all I can muster. "I'm not too familiar with a lot of fiction authors, but I'll definitely check out Kurt Bonsiget. I read mostly non-fiction."

"Really? have you read any Noam Chomsky?" The stranger asked.

"Um, no, I haven't read Noam Chauncy's stuff yet." I have to come clean with this lady before this gets out of hand. "To be honest I don't really read too often. And when I do it's usually a self-help book or something on money management. I just figured I'd swing in here and see if they had a cheap copy of *Catch-22*. A friend at work told me it's a must."

"I see. Well, for most of my life my home library was one shelf with four cookbooks on it. Then, when Nixon waged war on Vietnam, my father recommended I read *Catch-22*. So, I bought a copy. At first, reading was laborious, and I kept glancing at the page numbers hoping I had made more progress than just page 12. But then, after a little while, I forgot I was reading. I was engulfed. It probably sounds strange to hear, but it was as if I was experiencing the book. Sort of like when you watch a movie, you don't think about the fact that you are watching a movie, you're just sort of in the movie. Well the same thing happened to me with *Catch-22*. I read the entire book in just a couple days and craved more. That's when I read *Cat's Cradle* by Kurt Vonnegut.

"Anyway, I could go on and on, but from that day forward, I have been addicted to books. The power of the written word to marshal the mind and ignite the imagination is unlike anything I've ever experienced—and I lived through the sixties young man."

Well great. Now I have to buy the book. I thank the stranger for her testimony, purchase the book, and head home. That lady was right, reading is work. And every page takes so long to read. I'm never going to finish this tome. Several hours must have slipped by when hunger snapped me out of *Catch-22*'s pages. I was completely sucked in. That lady was right, this is something new.

Three days later, as soon as the bookstore opened (at 9:00 a.m. sharp), I rushed in and asked, "Where can I find *Catch Cradle* by Kurt Bonsiget? It's urgent."

The Bookshop

Rachel White

A trill of bell as I close the door
and then a hush. So still the air
in the sunny room where sits a girl
on a simple chair, reading from a book
open in her palm. A cat is curled
on the windowsill. I lose myself
in lines from Donne and disappear
in Yeats. Only a creak of the wooden
floor brings me back to time and place.
I wish I had nine lives and more
for marvelous worlds on every shelf.

Once Upon a Time at a Bookshop

Christine Fraizer

Outside the chilled shadows of early evening are closing down. Porch lights would soon flicker on, one by one along the neighborhood sidewalks, and mothers would call children into houses for brushing teeth and saying prayers before bed. Within the bookshop a girl approaches she will find light and warmth and breathe deeply a familiar scent, like leaves drying in autumn. This is a treasured place, her sanctuary, where comfort lingers in story books and an old man who scurries about his business mindful of his evening guests.

She enters. The bell rings. Brisk and obliging, the old man goes to the top shelf in a book case row of shelves just to the right of the shop's front desk. "Read this," he says softly, placing a book at the table where she sits.

She looks up at the old man.

"Why this?" she asks.

His face is luminous, and a dreamy look is in his eye.

"It's about a girl," he says, "and like you, she understands language of the heart."

The girl at the table holds the book in her hands, and studies the girl pictured on its cover. Her hair is in a ponytail and in her arms, she holds a pig. A goose stretches her neck above a fence rail and a sheep stands, not in the least intimidated by the beautiful large gray spider hanging by a thread over his head. The pig does not appear so sure, or maybe he stares in wonder.

She opens the book and inhales the fragrance of its pages. Clean. Crisp. And the promise of spring and a time she can gently pull the petals from a brown-eyed Susan. "He loves me. He loves me not." She would know her truth, an undeniable certainty, in the final petal. "He loves me."

He must.

The book she reads evenings, in the bookshop, at the table the old man reserves for her. The house, where she returns each night, is quiet, unlike a past of not so long ago trembling with raised voices, loud bangs, and slamming doors. She shelters under a tent of sheets dreaming of a spider, Charlotte, who because of an unselfish heart saves the life of the timorous pig Wilbur. She thinks of the girl with the pony tail, Fern, who sits on a milk stool listening to the talk of beloved farm animals.

"Wilbur was far too remarkable to surrender him, as are you," Fern whispers to the girl in her dreams. The girl knows not to despair of Charlotte's fate. She dies, and she has to, upon laying her eggs, but the youngsters hatch, several hundred of them. They thrive, some floating away on the breeze to build lives, others returning to embrace lives the winds had mistaken.

The girl understands. He will come back. He will say "my little girl," never again to leave her.

She feels it in her heart. She hears it in a spider's words to a pig she protected simply because of love and friendship and hope.

"Winter will pass, the days will lengthen, the ice will melt in the pasture pond. The song sparrow will return and sing, the frogs will awake, the warm wind will blow again. All these sights and sounds and smells will be yours to enjoy, Wilbur – this lovely world, these precious days."

The girl smiles reading the final page, once upon a time at a bookshop, where an old man recognized a story to soothe a little girl's tender heart.

The Bookshop

Kelly Henriod

When I'm feeling brave, I come to the bookshop.
Spines of colorful soldiers stand straight and stiff.
Ready for action.
Reporting for duty.
Legions of pages,
Braced for the dog-ears trained to assail them.
Bold volumes that contain
Concepts ripe for the conquering,
Characters waiting to make my acquaintance,
Messages poised to be unfurled.
Slide a book off its shelf like a sword from its sheath,
Let the battle commence.

Last Night at the Bookshop

Patrick de Freitas

I need to say right off that it wasn't really last night. It was really early this morning. And I also need to say right off that what happened wasn't really a crime. Not as far as I'm concerned.

I mean how can it be a crime to read?

Sometimes it's necessary and vital to a person's well-being to read. And if the only place you can find the right thing to read is in a bookshop and it's 3:30 in the morning and the bookshop doesn't open for hours and hours, how can it be a crime?

To break in, I mean. And read.

I know, I know, you're sitting there primly thinking, "what about online? The internet. You can find anything there. Entire novels."

But that's online. And that's the problem. That's what's wrong. Sure, the words line up in the proper order, the sentences all make sense in the way they're supposed to make sense, and there's a beginning and an end, just like with real books, with printed books.

But it doesn't smell the same online. It doesn't smell at all, except that weird electric plasticy smell computers and laptops and cell phones exude. Next time you're close to one, lean in. Take a whiff. They smell dumb. They don't smell of thought, of thoughtful design, of designed delight, of delightful stories on paper, of paper of a thousand subtle smells, of paper from a hundred trees, all a little different.

And it doesn't feel the same online. What does a keyboard feel like, after all? Just these little nubbins on the end of your fingers, jerking about on command. It's foolish to expect more. It's foolish to expect the weight of wisdom, the wisdom of humor, the humor of genius anywhere but in a printed book, a book with a certain heft, a certain feel, a certain quiet magic.

Well, you say, what about the books in your house. Nothing to read there? Nothing in the in pile, that gathering of high intent, of great ambitions, of clear failures of follow-through? Well, no, actually. Somehow essays on *Grape Juice & Solipsism* next to *The Conductor of Verisimilitude* next to Philip Larkin, he of the best poem in the world, next to *The Invention of Nature*, none of it made enough sense to be read. Not last night.

But last night at the bookshop, I found a book making sense.
So that's why I broke in. To read something. The details, the whys, the hows, the outwitting of the security devices, don't matter. Trust me, it's done. I covered my tracks well.

I'm sorry if it upsets you but really, I didn't take anything. Except satisfaction.

And anyway no one knows what happened last night at the bookshop. Just me. And I'm not telling.

The Thoughts of Avondale

Marcayla Weidenbacher

Dragons and bookstores go hand in hand (or talon in talon), one just has to make sure practically everything is fireproof. Believe me, more than once I have had my fur singed by a wayward dragon sneeze.

My name is Avondale, I am the Border Collie resident reading therapy dog and supervisor here at the Talons and Scales Bookstore. It's funny, but my dragon Tracia says that she's the owner / supervisor, but everyone here at the bookstore knows that I'm the one who is really in charge.

My duty as a reading therapy dog involves me sitting or lying in the center of the young reader's section every day for two hours, give or take, and having drakes and draklets read to me all while I get massaged and fed treats. It is a most wonderful therapy.

My job as the supervisor has much more variety but is a bit more hectic. Like for example, the holiday sales (actually any sale for that matter) are complete and total nightmares. You see, dragons have keen eyesight and are savvy bargain hunters, and when they spot a really good deal it's just best to stay out of their way...unless of course you WANT to get stepped on.

The poetry readings the bookstore hosts are by far much more mellow in nature, although I personally feel like poetry is more of a cat thing. Being the canine good citizen that I am, I still sit or lie down and politely listen to what the local poets have written for that particular month...unlike the Beagle, who at last month's reading booed every poet who came on stage.

Another low-key event that meets up about once a month is the book club. I don't really have too much to say about this event because usually once it starts I take a nap.

Book signings are always exciting, it's like a big party with lots of food, crowds, new smells, and did I already mention food? My most favorite part though is when cake and ice cream is being served and either some dragon forgets about their food or someone drops their plate, and when that happens it is also my duty as the Living Vacuum Cleaner to go and clean up the messes. Although, my efforts are not always appreciated at times.

If I were to make one change to the bookstore, I would have that gaudy crystal chandler that hangs above the central part of the store removed. The reason why I would have it removed is it seems like once a month the shiny fake strands of gems attract young dragons, and they fly up to the huge light fixture and get tangled up in it. Usually Tracia or one of the other employees fetches a ladder and gets the trapped dragon down while mama or papa dragon looks on with worry or is chewing out their offspring.

But there was this one particular time where a mama dragon took matters into her own claws and flew up to the chandler to free her drake. I don't think she thought her plan all the way through, because as soon as she got up there she immediately became ensnared by the crystalline threads of doom as well, making her and the drake looking like deranged Christmas ornaments as they swung through the air. Luckily, that incident had a happy ending.

All in all, working at the Talons and Scales Bookstore is enjoyable and I'd rather be here than anywhere else.

Once Upon a Time at the Bookshop

Didier Bouchever

As Alice walked to the bookstore down the street from her house she could still hear the chanting crowd ringing in her head, "HUMAN RIGHTS NOW! HUMAN RIGHTS NOW!"

As Chance leaves the bookstore for lunch he composes a little poem in his head:

"She is life.
She is love.
She is what we find out.
She is everything I dreamt about inside the trap.
I am ice water in the Nalgene.
I will find her one day,
and everything we lost."

Alice and Chance pass each other in the street.

Chance notices Alice's "RIGHTS HERE RIGHTS NOW" sticker and wishes she would hold his hand.

Alice notes Chance's copy of *Do Androids Dream of Electric Sheep* and wishes he would kiss her on the cheek.

Alice enters the bookstore just as it begins to rain. She sees a picture of Chance on the wall, "Employee of the Month," and hopes he will return soon. Then she strolls around the shop with hands clasped behind her back composing a little poem:

"Stricken with a flash
of calm inspiration,
the beauty of space
and great literature on tape;
the rain,
lazily drooling itself onto earth,
smells
overwhelming.
My feeling:
I'm finally home."

Chance orders a medium Coke and a large french-fry from Carl's Junior and writes down an idea he had for a TV show about a man who is color-blind, but only in the morning; at 12 noon every day the man can instantly see colors again resulting in hilarious hijinks and colorful situations.

Chance retrieves his bag of food and walks back to the bookstore. The sky opens up at that moment and begins to rain. He composes a little poem for the girl he saw in the street:

"I saw her,
clothed in nothing but sunshine,
from above and to the side,
she stretched her arm out and up
and locked her fingers
and closed her eyes really hard
then yawned
like a happy cat.
I wish I saw her last night dancing
in a grey dress.
I wish I saw her
Every day..."

Alice pulls a copy of Frank Herbert's *Dune* off a dusty shelf. The book is bound in red leather and smells like delicious wet earth. Alice kisses the book's spine.

Chance walks into the bookstore dripping wet. He sees Alice in the back, he sees her kiss the red book, and in a flash of courage and hope he walks straight up to her, but as Chance is about to tap the girl on the shoulder and ask her name she opens the beautiful old book and a bright flash of yellow light bursts out from the book and engulfs both Chance and Alice in its glow. They are both sucked inside the cover of the book.

The book lands with a thud on the ground.

Alice and Chance find themselves standing together on the blazing sands of an infinite scorching desert. Alice grabs Chance's hand as they look around in utter shock. Then their eyes meet; they squeeze each other's hands a little tighter, then, removing the masks to each other's Stillsuits, Chance leans over and kisses Alice on the cheek.

Alice smiles.

Little Oak Bookshop for Tiny People

Anya Ellahie

I woke up to the smell of morning dew and the sound of buzzing bees searching for flowers to pollinate. My eyes squinted as I glared at the sun. I knew it was time to get up. This was the day I had been waiting for—the opening of Little Oak Bookshop. I put on my best woolly blue dress and my matching boots and hurried to the table to have my breakfast - a crumb of bread and a dot of jam. As soon as I finished, I hurried to the door. The bitter wind swept my deep red hair into my face, but I did not care as I walked to the Everly pond and skipped my way across on pebbles. I hurried through petunias, tulips and several other flowers until I finally found my way to the bookshop.

The shop was bigger than I had ever imagined. They had already opened so I could walk in. I found many wonderful books like *Anne of Green Meadows* and *Harry Flotter*. I had just noticed the little café there, so I went to get a drink of a drop of honey, wonderful for a cold winter's day. I read many books but by the time I finished *Hollyanna* the bookshop was closing, and I had to go. I felt dismayed, but I knew the bookshop was open tomorrow and the day after that.

On the way home, I stopped at the butchers to get a piece of sausage for dinner. Then I stopped at Bartholomew Fresh Bee Honey to get a tin of honey for breakfast. When I got home, I slowly ate my sausage then took a nice warm bath, dried myself and changed into my nightgown. I crept into bed, pulled the covers over and I quickly fell asleep thinking warm thoughts of where I had been today.

The Traveling Bookstore

Iman Ellahie

The sound of jingling keys and the rattle of the doorknob ensured that the store was closed. A pair of green eyes flashed in the darkness. With an abnormal gust of wind, a pile of newly arrived books tumbled from the shipping box on to the floor. The pair of green eyes revealed a paw. With a small tap of claws a book fell off the shelf.

"Ouch!" called a small voice from the spot where the book had landed. "You could have at least tried to catch me. I think you injured my spine."

"That wasn't me. It was the small boy who was reading you today," said the green eyes. "He nearly ripped one of my pages, I would have had to pay the R.P.B.I," said the small voice.

"The Ripped Pages Book Insurance?" asked the green eyes questioningly.

"Yes, precisely" cried the small voice.

The small voice was in fact the essence or soul of the book. This book was *The Very Hungry Caterpillar*. She was always worried about something or another.

"Enough chitchat. We have to wake up the others otherwise we won't have time to travel," said the green eyes. They both slowly started to tap various books. The green eyes tapped books as if he knew all of them by heart. The Very Hungry Caterpillar on the other hand tapped an array of random books. After a while the green eyes called out for The Very Hungry Caterpillar to stop.

“I think we have enough for today,” said the green eyes. The essences of many books had been called upon and they were excitedly awaiting the information about where they would be traveling. The green eyes waited for the voices to cease and then he started talking.

“Today I will not tell you where we are traveling.” There was silence and then the green eyes pulled a book off a dusty shelf. It was way up high, so nobody bothered ever looking there. The green eyes opened the book to a page and tapped it with his paw. Then he chanted, “Once upon an Ocean Bookstore.” He chanted this again and the third time round the rest of the books joined in.

With a blinding light the room slowly started to spin, books flew off the shelves and then started to crumble on top of one another. As quickly as it had started everything disappeared and the books were no longer in the store. They were swimming in the deep blue ocean. A light up ahead indicated their destination. The books swam to the light, soon learning that it was a cave. As they swam into the cave, they noticed Merfolk with colorful tails of every design and pattern swimming about. Some had their noses in a book while others were just talking amongst themselves. There were fish and stingrays mingling about and new faces and friendships were brewing. There was even a shark looking at a seafood cookbook. The books watched with fascination until only two Merfolk were left.

“It’s time to head back,” called the green eyes. All the books took one last glance at the store as it would never look like this again. This was a magical traveling bookstore and it would be somewhere new by tomorrow. The books held hands and they were once again back in their own bookstore. The books fit back into their shelves and the green eyes prowled off for it was nearly opening time and they could not be seen wandering the store—till tonight!

The Wonderful Hat

Zahara Dockx-Wunderli

There was a magnificent hat. It was a sunny yellow with little blue ribbons and peacock feathers on top. A rich woman owned it and she was very proud about it. But that hat was no ordinary hat. If you put it on, incredible things will happen. Let's see what they are.

One fine day Lady Rose (the rich lady) was having tea. She was worried. She was of course wearing the hat.

"What can I do?" she thought.

"How am I supposed to know?" said a voice in her head. Rose jumped.

"Who said that?" she asked with a quiver.

No answer. She tried again. Nothing. Then she got an idea.

"Who is it?"

"It's me, your favorite hat. The best of all hats. The jewel of the sun."

"My hat? Impossible. I must be crazy." Rose thought in disbelief.

"Crazy?! Just because one of the most beautiful hats is talking to you. I am outraged!"

At that moment a servant came in and said "Miss Rose, it's time for your walk." Lady Rose hurried out of the room feeling a little confused. The sun was shining but it wasn't hot. The perfect day. But Rose didn't see it.

"Look at the sun shining. Feel the breeze."

"How do you know, you don't have eyes." said Rose in surprise.

"I feel." said the hat. "But you can feel and see. Do it."

Rose felt and saw. For the first time she saw the sun, for the first time she felt the wind. She was happy. She walked enjoying her hat, enjoying the wind, enjoying the sun.

"Oh, smell that smell of bread from the bakery." said the hat.

"How can you smell?"

"I feel. But you can see, feel, and smell." said the hat.

So, Rose smelled and smelled. She loved it. "I think I am going to buy some bread." So, she walked in enjoying her hat, enjoying the wind, enjoying the sun, enjoying the smell.

When Rose entered the bakery, she saw the baker. A plump man with blond hair. "Oh, Lady Rose! You don't come here very often." said the baker.

"Oh, I decided I could pay a visit and buy some bread." While Rose was looking for some good bread she saw a big jar of delicious looking candy displayed on the counter. Some boys were looking at the jar rather sadly. They were very skinny.

"Why don't you buy that jar of candy. Like that they will be happy." said the hat.

Lady Rose, now knowing how the hat knew went to the baker and said, "that big jar of candy and this loaf of good bread please." She gave the jar to the boys who were very happy. They said continuous thank-yous and hugs then they were off.

"Why don't you take that bread to your friend you haven't seen for many years. I think she is in the park feeding the birds like you used to when you were small."

So, Lady Rose went to the park enjoying her hat, enjoying the sun, enjoying the wind, enjoying the smell, enjoying kindness.

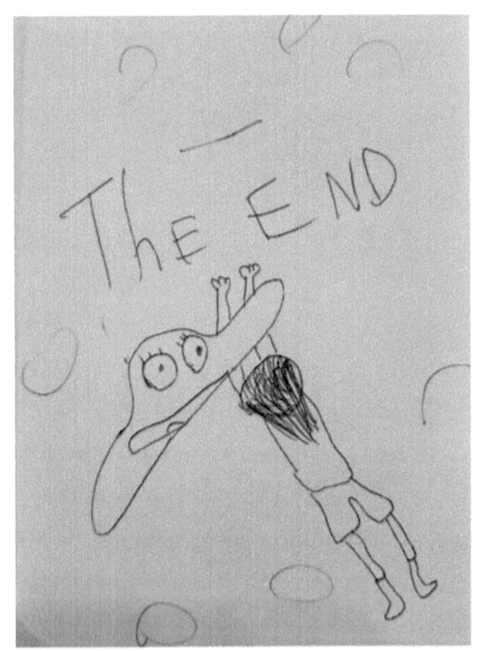

She got to the park and sat on a bench. Then she saw a pretty lady feeding the birds. She looked sad. Rose went to her. The lady looked extremely happy. So, they hugged each other both of them wordless. Rose said, "Here we are reunited and happy thanks to a wonderful hat." And the hat was happy too.

The Face on the Jacket of the Book

Brenda Sue Cowley

"Oh, my my... that is one of my faaaaavorites! Are you reading it for the third, possibly fourth time?"

Chloe looked up from her seated position on the floor of the bookshop to see a smiling, slightly stooped, older gentleman with wisps of grey hair poking out from underneath his old-fashioned hat. He was speaking to her with such giddiness, she couldn't help but giggle. He was staring at the book in her hands.

"No. But... I love his other stories, so I'm super excited for this one." The man dropped what seemed to be a cane, and quietly clapped his hands together. "So exciiiiiiting!"

Chloe took in his strange appearance. He wore a suit that made him look almost childlike, and a round eyeglass was placed over one jubilant eye and attached to a golden chain. His hat, askew, couldn't seem to decide if it should stay on his head or not. Between the business with the cane, the eye glass falling out, and the unstable hat, Chloe formed a true affection. He seemed familiar, the way some people feel real in a dream.

"I've never heard of this one," Chloe whispered, caressing the book.

The man leaned in a bit at this point. He replaced the eyeglass which promptly popped back out, the cane landed softly against the chair, and his hat bounced off of his head as he chortled, "I know you'll love it, because I wroooooote it!" And with this, he arranged his items, stood straight and proud and tilted his chin in a way that gave Chloe another gale of giggles—perhaps a little too loud, but she wanted to play along in case he was an actor hired to sell books.

"I'm sorry, sir, and I don't mean to be rude, but..." a tiny cough caught in her throat as she tried to explain. "This novel was first published in 1929 --"

"--Yes! Yes!" The man agreed with so much enthusiasm that the hat, eye-glass and cane went slipping away again.

"... and, um..." Chloe paused, "the author must be, well... dead."

"Well, I wrote it and I'm certainly not dead, or I wouldn't be standing here talking with a child..." The man broke off and reached for the book. Chloe handed it to him and watched, mystified as the book shimmered for a brief moment and then fell through the man's open palms to the floor with a fuhwomp!

"But I'm..." the man sputtered.

"Dead," blurted Chloe, staring at the book on the floor of the bookshop.

"No, I'm..."

"So dead. Like, a really long time." The book had landed face-down. The man looked at the palms of his hands.

"As a doornail," Chloe added. "I don't actually know what that means, other than you're really quite...dead."

And with that, it occurred to Chloe that she was not afraid of this man at all, even though he was the first real ghost she'd ever met.

"I'll be back tomorrow," Chloe whispered. "You wait for me here!"

"Why?" asked the man, with a furtive glance around the bookshop.

"Because you must not be finished," she said.

"Finished with what?"

"Writing!" Chloe winked, and hurried away, while the man stared at the face on the jacket of the book, just out of his reach on the floor of the bookshop.

Perfect Pet

Kayla Lien

Once, I was a princess
I was raised with manners and poise
And quite little choice
But I was no different from the rest

Older and older, still I grew
Now too big for my tower
They didn't want me to know of my power
So they kept me quiet and taught me to sew

I got older
And I got bolder
Started using ink
To say what I think

I started to write
They said, "Ladies don't do that.
You'll be scorned and laughed at.
Don't let your name fall into plight."

With a rage and a riot
I said, "This is who I am and what I want.
This is something I'm going to flaunt."
Let them try to keep me silent

They were beyond furious

"Princesses aren't creators,"
Scolded my berators
"Don't you care what will become of us?"

"Do you want your people to see you as weak?
Or our neighbors to see you as easy?"
Though the thought did make me queasy
I don't believe my future will be so bleak

I am no perfect princess up on your shelf
I am a knight
Who uses words to fight
and I am saving myself

Once upon a time at the bookshop...

Adelaide Gassman and Everett Gassman

I walked inside during a warm afternoon and looked at some books. Some I liked, some I didn't, some were ok, and some were strange. There was one book that I saw a woman reading. It was a small, old book. Suddenly, the woman threw it into a basket labeled 'free books.' I took it out and looked at it. It was old, but in great condition. I asked the woman, "What's wrong with it?"

"Strange things have happened to the owners of the book. Used to be my sister's but she left us. So, I brought it here and since no one's bought it. So I have no choice but to put in the free books bin, she said.

"What do you mean by strange things?" I asked.

"Well for instance 20 years ago, my sister bought it and the next day, she was gone! We've never seen her since. We guessed she moved or something happened to her," the woman said.

"Oh well. I'd like to purchase the book," I said.

"It's free," she said.

So, I took the book and left the shop. I opened the book and read the first few pages. It was about a girl who left her family. I turned the page and saw that the girl was in the book!!! She was with a lot of other people with a sign that said, "HELP!"

Zoe's Adventure in Lapotia

Lauren Ashley Kirton

Once upon a time at the bookshop on 42nd street, the owner, Suzy, was getting ready to open her bookshop. But this was no ordinary bookshop; it was the "Queen's English" bookshop. It was the biggest bookshop in the whole entire city of Quebec! This was a very big day for the "Queen's English." The very famous author, Mark Brown, was coming to present his new series, Latopia. Ring Ring! Suzy walked over to answer the phone. "Hello? Oh, Hi Mark Brown. Is there something wrong? Yes. You want to change the pricing of the books to $25.99 instead of $20.99? Of course. I will do that right away, sir." answered Suzy.

On her way to the "Queen's English" Zoe was very excited to meet the author, Mark Brown. He was Zoe's favorite author in the whole wide world. "Hmmmmmh. I wonder what he looks like in person? Will he look anything like my posters of him?" said Zoe. As Zoe approached the "Queen's English" Zoe thought to herself, "I just love the "Queen's English."

After two hours of waiting in line, Zoe was finally able to get a signed book of Latopia. As Zoe was leaving the shop, she couldn't wait to get home to read the book. She started to run home but tripped. She hit her head very hard. She was starting to feel very very dizzy. Her head fell to the ground.

As Zoe awoke, she could only see cornfields that stretched for miles. "This isn't Quebec. Where am I?" said Zoe. Her heart started to pump a lot faster. She began to panic. "Wait. Calm down. I can figure something out." Zoe thought to herself. Then Zoe noticed that the book, Latopia was on the ground. Zoe picked up the book and skimmed the first page. "I think I just got sucked into the book. The first page talks about a girl who got sucked into a book. She could only see cornfields." Thought Zoe. The feeling of panic started to come to her again.

As she kept reading, realization came to her face. "I have to do the things in the book to reach the end," exclaimed Zoe. According to the book, she had to follow the sun that always stayed in the east. It would then lead her to the Swampy Wampy river. Then, she would have to climb to the top of Mt. Olympia, where she will meet this, Gweedo. He will tell her how to get home.

Zoe set off for the Swampy Wanpy River. After two hours of walking through cornfields, Zoe made it to the river. Zoe noticed that the river was actually a river of a gooey substance. She had to jump across on moss-covered rocks. "This was going to be easy" she thought. As Zoe approached the last rock, she slipped and fell into the gooey water. "Ewwww!" Zoe pulled herself out from the water. As she looked up, she could see the mountain.

After hours of climbing, Zoe finally approached the top. Tired, sore, and covered in goo from the river, Zoe comes upon a man who had his back turned from her. As she approached him, he turned around. At first, she noticed his bright orange hair and beard. Next, his emerald green eyes. Then his robes of astonishing color. He then introduced himself as Gweedo. As Zoe was about to speak, Gweedo snapped his fingers and she suddenly awoke on her couch at home with the book on the table.

Woman

Elsha Gallegos-Fukuda

I Am a Beautiful Jewel
In the Crown of Humanity.
I Am an Irreplaceable Sculpture
In the Gallery of Life.
I Am a Treasured Flower
In the Garden of Nature.
I Am an Intelligent Computer
In the Technology of Time.
I Am a Wonderful Rainbow
In the Skies of Space.
I Am a Precious Child
In the Cradle of Earth.
I Am a Vital Force
In the Perfect Universe.
I Am a Mysterious Being
In the Womb of the World.
Behold! Me! Woman! In All her Splendor!

Untitled

Maggie Elizabeth Godman

I've spent the last hour browsing at my favorite bookstore, trying to decide between a historical fiction novel and a mystery. Finally, I decide. Both.

As I walk past the children's room, I spot a little redhead, half running, half stumbling, across the room, carrying a book bigger than she is. She stops at her father who is sitting on the floor and plops both herself and the book into his lap. A smile spreads across my face. I think back to being 4 years old and going to the bookstore with my mom to pick up an Eloise book, then again at 6 to get some Junie B. Jones books. When I was 8 I remember waiting at home, my nose pressed up against the cool glass of my bedroom window waiting for my dad to get home after he had stood in line for hours to get me the newest Harry Potter book. My teenage years were the beginning of my romance obsession. No matter how many swoon-worthy books I read I still wanted more. The meet cute, the first kiss, the declaration of undying love. The conflict, the resolution, the happily ever after.

As much as I loved my romance books and my fictional boyfriends, I didn't date much. I got tongue-tied too easily, and meeting people in real life wasn't anything like meeting someone on the pages of a novel. I didn't go out much, at least not in the way you'd think. I traveled to Narnia, I cliff-jumped in Forks, Washington, I took potions class at Hogwarts, spent an entire summer catching monkeys in the Cherokee Ozarks, and once held hands with Boo Radley himself. I'd been everywhere, seen everything.

The little girl's laugh pulls me back from my thoughts and I glance at the clock. I should finish up and head to pay but before I do that I want to take one last peek at the bargain table. There sitting right on top, in plain sight, is one of my favorite books! I run my hands across the cover and my heart skips a beat. This book changed everything for me. This book was the first present my now-husband ever gave me. He bought it for me on our first date, and when I told my mom about it she smiled and said, "You're going to marry him aren't you?". Seven months later we were engaged, three months after that we were saying "I do."

Now a couple years later I know without a shadow of a doubt that our love is greater than all the fictional love stories I've ever read.

As I make my way to check out with my pile of books I feel a tug at my sweater. The little redheaded girl beams up at me, her crooked smile and head of curls making my heart ache. Her dad scoops her up and leans in towards me, kissing me on the forehead. "Ready?" he asks knowing that I would spend another three hours here if I could. I shake my head yes and grab his hand. "I'm ready. I say, "You ready, Charlotte?" I see her eyes glisten, she's definitely taking after me when it comes to her love of bookstores. My husband wipes the lone tear rolling down her cheek. "Don't worry little spider, we'll be back."

Books change you, they shape and mold you. That book my husband gave me ended up changing my life, that book was the beginning of our once upon a time.

Real Friends

Bretton Newman

Once upon a time there were two little girls and they were neighbors. Their friendship bloomed from a very young age because they lived next door to each other and played

together often. They made blanket forts and lemonade stands. They had sleepovers. They told each other secrets and made a telephone out of orange juice cans that they tried to stretch between their homes. They were close at times and needed space at times. They knew each other intimately and they loved each other.

They liked to explore their neighborhood and ventured out often on foot or bicycle to The King's English Bookshop around the corner from their homes. The girls met real authors at TKE. They listened to countless books read to them from a very young age until they began to read to each other and spend quiet time

reading on their own. They pretended to write and publish books. They even had a laminating machine to laminate the finished copies of their stories. They had fights and they made up. They loved each other. They were Real Friends.

TKE

John McCullough

Every culture has a place where people meet, talk, renew acquaintances, exchange news – and gossip – and by these actions create a community. In Ireland it is the village pub. In Mexico it is the Sunday plaza stroll. Salt Lake City has a similar institution, the independent bookstore, a kind of intellectual pub where we may gather, renew acquaintance with the familiar and friendly bookstore personnel and customers who are also our neighbors or friends from work.

The King's English is one of these intellectual oases where we may meet, find a good new—or old—book and see again the people who make up our community. The bookstore personnel are pretty constant – people we have known for years, who know us and what we like to read. I moved into the neighborhood in 1976, so we have grown into close neighbors together. TKE is a community treasure that has nourished so many good things for us, from story-time for our children, to sponsoring visits from truly treasured local, national and international authors, to selling books at the Hibernian Society's annual Night with the Irish Poets (when The King's English Becomes the King's Irish!).

While TKE is such an integral part of our local community, it is known –famous, if you will - in every independent bookstore in the country as I found out last week in Powell's in Portland. I wish it not 40 more years but the 400 it so richly deserves!!

Just a Thought

Louis Borgenicht

Back in the old days, that would be the '60s (I had graduated from high school in 1960), paperbacks were very different from the way they are today. Not just in price: I discovered a copy of Sophie's Choice published in 1979 on my bookshelf at a cost of $3.40. These days paperbacks are priced at a minimum of $16.

The most dramatic change is that paperbacks are larger today; back in the '60s their size was approximately 4x7", a nice compact handleable size. It was even possible to fit them into a jacket pocket.

Most of the paperbacks on my shelves are testimony to my purchases over the past forty-six years. The other day however I discovered an old copy of Lonesome Dove, a book that most of my friends had read but I had not. It was 4x7" and I decided to read it. Since it is 947 pages and I usually read for five minutes before falling asleep I figure it could take me the rest my life to read it.

The other major difference between the paperbacks of the '60s and 2017 is that some paperbacks had a distinct pleasant smell back then, as if they were fresh off the printing press. I thought it was the ink. The best were Bantam paperbacks; Signet and Ballentine were odorless. When you opened a new Bantam paperback there was an odiferous thrill...you knew you had just purchased a new paperback every time you opened it.

But the copy of Lonesome Dove I had chosen to read had been printed in 1985 and was without any odor. It was a sad but necessary reality. I had just been to a concert by James McMurtry, Larry's son, and recalled that I had a copy of the book on my shelf. After I started reading it my paperback past came to the fore.

The choice of what to read is interesting. I have a plethora of unread books on my shelf, purchased from The King's English usually on a whim and few of them paperbacks. Several years ago I bought a Kobo thinking I might get into reading on a tablet, but I tried and found I missed the heft of a real book. Having hidden the Kobo in a drawer with other obsolete electronic media I reverted to checking my bookshelves in search of a new book.

There is a certain reward in perusing my shelves for unread books. A pleasure at having purchased them in expectation and the knowing I would rediscover them when the perfect time arrived.

The Great American Eclipse

Dean Hall

I didn't know that a total solar eclipse was on my bucket list, but as I listened to all the hype, an urge started to grow in my belly and only got stronger as the date approached. I got online, charted the path, and found that St. Matthews, South Carolina was dead center in the path of totality. A major concern was all that traffic, but St. Matthews is off the beaten path, and I thought we could reach it using back roads.

Our car has a navigation system, and Linda has an app on her smartphone. We used both, (to have a second opinion) sometimes following one and sometimes the other. We passed through a military reservation and noticed several diamond shaped warning signs for TANK CROSSING. We also like to look for unusual church names. While crisscrossing the back roads of America, we've come across some pretty unusual names. Today was no exception as we came across Horse Stamp Church in rural Georgia. For the next half hour, we tried to come up with some explanation as to why a church would be called Horse Stamp?

We pulled into St. Matthews about 1:30. A few blocks down the road I noticed cars parked in the three stalls of an abandoned car wash. The people there had folding chairs and solar glasses. Ah, solar glasses! Before leaving Florida, I had tried in vain to find some. I guess those glasses all went to other parts of the country. We did bring along some cardboard with a small hole, a pinhole camera. It was better than nothing. I pulled in, rolled down the window, and asked if anyone had an extra pair. To my surprise, the answer was, yes! So, this was where we stopped.

The total eclipse was over an hour away. Isolated fluffy clouds drifted across the sky. I brought out our cooler and folding chairs, and Linda handed me the glasses. My first view took my breath away. The partial eclipse had already begun. A perfectly smooth black arc had started to nibble away at the sun. Even though I knew what to expect, it was still a shock. For over an hour the moon continued to eat away at the sun. Linda and I took turns with the glasses. The clouds blew away, and the sky became perfectly clear. I thought it would gradually grow darker, but it stayed quite bright until just before totality. Insects started to chirp, and birds started to call to each other. I watched as the final wink of sunlight disappeared.

It lasted over two and a half minutes. Stars appeared in the sky. We no longer needed the glasses. It continued to grow darker. Blocks away we could hear people cheering. But it passed all too quickly. Then the first spark appeared. It caused a flash in my field of vision, and without the glasses, I had to glance away. People around us called it "the diamond ring."

In the morning, we used I-95 for our return trip. Along the way we saw a sign for an upcoming exit. It said, "Horse Stamp Church Road." Linda went bananas. She immediately did some research on her phone. It turns out that during the Civil War, soldiers in this area sometimes met together for worship services. This was either out in the open or under the trees. Before the service, they used their horses to flatten the grass. Many years later, a church was built that retained the name. Mystery solved. At least that's the story.

Valen Choinard

Riley Chouinard

anonymous

Jesse Colby

Contributors

Chaunceton Bird

Chaunceton Bird is an attorney in Salt Lake City, Utah. He is also a writer, and is the author of an award-winning academic article, several short stories, and the forthcoming novel Malibu Motel (Zero Books, 2019).

Lou Borgenicht, M.D.

LB is a retired pediatrician, blues harp player (Better Off With the Blues), standup comedian, writer and a participant in Old Coots Giving Advice (a help stand at the Saturday Farmer's Market). He has written over 200 letters to the editor and is currently deciding whether to shred or publish them in a book. He has been unable to read Anna Karenina despite compulsive urging from Jan Sloan. This summer, however, he is plowing through Hawaii by James Michener, despite the fact that he had to purchase a copy from Barnes and Noble. He has no guilt for anything he is either able or not able to do.

Valen Chouinard

Valen Chouinard has been an artist since a very young age. Both musically and artistically gifted, she has had many opportunities to display her gifts and talents. In fifth grade, she placed in the annual PTA reflections contest. In sixth grade, she placed first in a music composition competition. Now she is striving to one day make a living off of her artwork. She has experimented with many different mediums of art but has found comfort in drawing and painting. She plans on taking more advanced art classes in the future.

Jessie Colby

Jesse Colby is a designer, illustrator and art director who loves making books. While artist in residence at University of Utah's Book Arts Program, Colby wrote and illustrated Adrift in the Days: living in, and in between, holidays.

Brenda Sue Cowley

Brenda Sue Cowley has been living, performing, and writing, (among other things), in Salt Lake City since 1991. Originally from Portland, Oregon, Brenda found her creative voice and community while living in Salt Lake City. She's grateful to The King's English for encouraging her to continue to explore her voice through the written word, and is thrilled with this most recent publication.

Patrick de Freitas

A Westerner by choice, Patrick de Freitas was born and raised in the UK. For reasons that are sometimes unclear to him, he lives in Salt Lake City.

Anya and Iman Ellahie
Anya Ellahie lives in Salt Lake City with her parents and older sister. She enjoys reading Harry Potter books, writing stories and drawing. She hopes to write, illustrate and publish her own books one day. She loves visiting The King's English Bookshop and looking at new books to read. She also enjoys baking sweet treats with her sister and father. Iman Ellahie lives in Salt Lake City, Utah with her family. Since moving to Utah from London two years ago, she has developed a passion for skiing. She loves to draw, dance, bike, rock climb and hang out with her friends. Her favorite book series, so far, are The Hunger Games and Legend trilogies, the Divergent quartet and of course, Harry Potter. She is a seventh-grade student at Rowland Hall and loves going to all her classes.

Christine Fraizer
Chris Fraizer continues to write pages as King's English continues to turn them. While her day job involves writing stories about real people and events, she prefers writing about fictional people and events during her

off time. In the process, she has grown quite fond of characters she hopes come alive for readers.

Elsha Gallegos-Fukuda
Elsha grew up in Salt Lake. She lives with her husband and her son in Layton. She loves poetry and literature. She loves spending time with her family and they enjoy many activities such as hiking, biking, reading, and movies. Her favorite places in the world are Monterey, California and Ketchum/Sun Valley, Idaho.

Dean Hall
Dean enjoys yard work, live performances, and is an avid reader with an extensive personal library. He earns a living as a computer programmer, but deep down inside, he's always wanted to be a pirate.

Russ Isabella
Russ has been an avid reader for much of his life and a King's English groupie for 30 of those years.In his spare (i.e., non-reading) time, Russ is a University of Utah professor of Human Development and a professional sport photographer.

Hartman Macey

Hartman is a bookseller with a keen interest in books/poetry that examines, or has a strong sense of, ancestry and nature. He's a bit of a Luddite, and loves the cold, he believes it increases his capacity to write things he cares about.

Kayla Lien

Kayla Lien is a high school sophomore, and an avid supporter of sweatpants and hoodies. She enjoys the smell of rain, hot chocolate, and old books. If you looked through her camera roll, the only thing on there would be pictures of the sky and of her dog. Kayla tries to look intimidating, but her 5-foot stature doesn't do much to help. Often, you will find Kayla lying on her bed, sitting underneath a table, or hiding from her homework and responsibilities.

Samuel Morse

Samuel Morse would rather hang out with his friends than write, but he would rather write than practice the piano. Accordingly, he is an accomplished writer and average pianist. In search of less snow and more sweet tea, he moved to Tennessee in the summer of 2018, where he resides with his two dogs, Perry and Sparky - the inspirations for Tails of a Bookstore.

Bretton Newman

Bretton Newman relocated to Utah from New York and settled a few blocks from The King's English in 1999. Bretton's favorite poet is Mary Oliver and her daughter Ella enjoys reading graphic novels like Real Friends.

Marcayla Weidenbacher

Marcayla Weidenbacher hails from West Valley City, Utah and is the proud pet parent of a Border Aussie named Shu. A weaver of tales since she could talk, Marcayla is currently writing the first book of her YA fantasy series.

Rachel White

Rachel White grew up in Ogden, Utah making special trips to the King's English, then studied economics and poetry at the University of Utah. She lives near the Red Iguana in the Guadalupe neighborhood of Salt Lake City.

www.ingramcontent.com/pod-product-compliance
Lightning Source LLC
Chambersburg PA
CBHW032126050726
47590CB00008B/2984